Bone

Hunting

Bone Hunting
© Trinity Catlin/ Cathexis Northwest Press

No part of this book may be reproduced without written permission
of the publisher or author, except in reviews and articles.

First Printing: 2024

ISBN: 978-1-952869-88-4

Cover Design by Audrey Shepard
Editing & Design by C. M. Tollefson
Cathexis Northwest Press
cathexisnorthwestpress.com

Bone

Hunting

Trinity Catlin

Cathexis Northwest Press

Bone

Hunting

Even in the open form of the table of contents, we are pulled into the haunted suspension of Trinity Catlin's debut chapbook, *Bone Hunting*, where an attentive alertness combines with gorgeous metaphor and a trail of heartbreaking insights on a path toward wholeness and clear-eyed love.

Woven into the mix: our changing earth and its perils and wonders, a bow or two toward writing from art, a bit of allusion (yes, that *is* an albatross!), and the many webs of eros and danger we might encounter in intimacy. I'm thrilled to invite you, dear reader, to enter the realm of this confident, inspiring new voice, which has so regularly amazed me in these last few years. Here, an embrace of the elliptical is matched by a precision of vision, a prodigious aesthetic sophistication grounded by a deep sense of a morality that transcends the merely human, whether in the discomfiting acceptance of invading ants or the early life decision—to prize antlered life over the chance to take a "good shot"—that comes at the end of the title poem. Above all, the discovery and celebration of uniqueness—as writer and as human—makes its mark on every illuminating page.

—Sarah Maclay

Table of contents

Carmel: Lavinia	1
Somewhere Else	3
Heartline	5
Antarctica	6
The Argument of Snow	7
Ways to Kill the Belladonna of Sadness	11
Figure, Oil on Canvas, a Mirror	13
To the Ants in my Kitchen	14
Three Rivers: Fawn Head Mantle	15
Bone Hunting	16
Here and There	18
Mount Washington: Rain for the Departing	20
Kiss by the Window	22
Delivering the End	23

Carmel: Lavinia

I press a book into my cheek.

Words embedded in tissue.

                  Quiet,

except for the breath of the shoreline.

The story goes:

        Lavinia is a landscape.

No,

        the Earth is a tongue and two severed hands
        baked in clay. Butter coating its thick crust.

Today,

driftwood touched by wildfire
emerges from the sand as
            blots of ink
    on a thin page,
    and I cannot write it
    better than the ocean.

The narrative is in soil, coal,
                    wheat,
                        cattle.

In the legacy of Spaniards,
        and the Mission,
               and their God.

In the gates around town
        —ribs around a verdant heart—
            in pearl encrusted pillars,
    the refrain to citrus and rest,

>   in his entitlement to my body,
>   in my gut.

I cannot tell this story better than the ground.

On the shore,

>   I hear a warbling,
>   the trill of a child and their kite,
>   a bird somewhere far,
>   a story about Jeffers and the hawk,
>   the delta emptying into the sea.

God,
>   I'm afraid,
>   that I'm missing something.

Somewhere Else

Grant me the serenity to accept

    the cavity that is spading into my molar.
    The father's shovel that takes a knife to
    the soil's tongue,
    the peeling of a sunburn,
    the petri-shoulder,
    the calcitic trees,
    knowing you sublingually.

    Let me accept the shovel
    as it cracks open my jaw,
    as it uses my bones as
    fencing for my lungs,
    as you bury seeds in
    the open well where
    my heart used to be,
    where a graveyard
    of quiet mornings lives.

    "Accepting" is cold lemonade
    on a hot porch, or dinner
    with our old friends. Your
    hand on the small of my
    back, thumbing at my spine.
    These things—

The things I cannot change,

    The black walnut tree
    stretching its fingers
    to the sky, the piles
    of bruised strawberries,
    Big Sur, Coney Island, and
    your proud heavy footsteps.
    Your voice as it coddled the
    wavering park boats.
    How

the courage to change the things I can

    lives in plumes of spring air,
    in sediment, sand, silica, magnesia,
    in Antarctica, or the mountains,
    in the lifeline of your palms,
    tracing out where to find the
    rest stop, tracing out where
    I can find your shape of blur.
    Courage is being anywhere
    but here,

and the wisdom to know the difference

    between taking medicine and dying
    was something you taught me.
    I am melting flesh down to the plum pit.
    I am eating fruit off the vine.
    I am rinsing my hands again and again.

    But somewhere else,
    you and the hills gasped for air.
    Flushing green,
    rushing to bloom,
    to flower
    —to you.

Heartline

I.

Her water-hand. Narrow and long. Fingers curling inward to hide the language of the palm. Don't hurt me. The pleasure is in the idea. Her pointed nails. Picking at the scab till it's raw. Wrinkling. The lifeline pointing to a hidden interior.

II.

Tonight, the shore sends stars back to the sky. Bonfires scatter across dampened sand. She takes one end of a thin blanket and lays it down with precision—presses her shoes to its corners. Her tender thumb pulling your chin to her lips. She stares at the sound of waves—the absence of the ocean. Tonight a body is a fire, but you keep your hands to yourself.

III.

Yearning is a lesson unlearned by her teeth.

IV.

It might have been the grass, or the timbre of her voice. Hives reply, respond to a character assessment. Someone writes about the origin of an addict. Someone surrenders.

V.

Tomorrow, an answer will breed in my windpipe—in the confines of my bed. The walls will be close and untouchable. Ridges in the plaster will cluster in pale sickly cysts, and teach my skin how to speak in complete sentences. Knuckles along my spine. All I want is to talk to her—to place my palm into her hands.

Antarctica

The shelf swells out of the water. A wall of mirrors
fracturing against converging oceans.
Cape Horn at the backs of ice plates
that ration the memory of standing on an older
                                                               Earth.

    That is why we've traveled here.

Digging our heels into the blue desert. Cobalt skin
wrapped in dense wool, trudging along the funeral
continent. You learn to shepherd ice dunes. I am
waiting for disease to melt out of the land. As the
shelves crumble behind our tracks, we only consider
farther south. The albatross never appears, or lingers.
Wind exhausts the crystalline fields, sewn
together by desolation, by forgetfulness.
There is a silence that transposes
thought, and the white plains
somehow close in.
I have to hold
you. Look
deeper into
the tundra,
the clay
of my body
freezes
against
your purpose.
The naked candle drips along your down coat.

We shall stick it out to the end,
but we are getting weaker...
and the end cannot be far.

The Argument of Snow

Premise 1

Snow is falling: a memory
        now melting in my palms,
collecting on the lawn the way a throat closes,
            the way a lymph node swells under
        the pressure of an inside voice.

Fur-soaked. My mother's dog bites
                at my wrist
and barks at the snowflakes
            framing the front yard:
              a littering of quotation marks
        around a light-
polluted evening.

From the doorway,   my mother
        defends the dog   from the cold
through a series of commands
            she used to preserve
                for me.

        We watch snow
            fall   for the first time
in 16 years.   For a moment,

        I'm unsure
whether it's pouring   down,

        or if I'm being pulled
                up.
                  ……

Premise 2:

Watered down,
        nothing sticks.
December clings to spring,
        its chill gripping
                the windowsill.

      His bedsheets slope down
            his paused,   ridged pair of shoulders,
and I drip slowly   off the cliffed mattress,
          and out his front door—

    drenched, searching
        for traces of snow

in bruises of mud
      along the sidewalk,   along the neck,

in the damp bark of a pine tree,
      the leaves weighed down with water,
      the branches bowing towards the earth:
          a swan hooking its neck
                towards the mouth
                      of a flightless bird.

Then it appears
    in a set of teeth on
        the inner thigh,
in an argument
    about Black Sabbath
    and nihilism,
in my hips
    when they become a rhetorical question,

in the moment
    I watched him tumble
out of love   with me, as he
    scraped the wet
        shirt off my
shoulder,   punished the cotton

    blend,   and saw in my skin
how deeply   I love the cold,
how I couldn't
   make us
     warm again.
             ……

There used to be a field of snow,
    stretching till vision blurred,
a cheek in velvet pink, a thumb
    caressing the hillside
—hushed, lulled,
    tracing fresh trails
    carved by your breath,
a stream slipping
    from the inner eye, cradled
between mountain peaks,
   a pulse: felt, silent,
beating beneath ice,
    the ground unthawed,
    a blistered heel
      painting the snowbank red:
    all the colors of craving
    —of knowing absence.

Back then, I remembered
    more than glimpses
   of your crooked teeth,
the slow drum   of your words,
   the candle lit
    beside your portrait.
You stayed settled on the lawn—
   our hands frozen
in the direction of morning,
your face: gentle,
   exposed,
     blemished.
There used to be
   an argument:

The snow lingered,
             desired
         a sun to rage
                 against
         —a form.

Ways to Kill the Belladonna of Sadness

I.

Read her his script. A mutilated first impression. Her name grafted onto legs wrapped around his waist, onto legs dripping along the slick hot shower tiles. Her name—legs and river-blood. Her green-eyed rage against his metamour—a fire tempered by saliva in place of water. The dogs are men, who are dogs, who are people who have made her naked again. She will ask for something terrible to happen.

> NOTE: "Name" is a sheer white dress.
> Burn it if necessary.
> He is an artist.

II.

An open bedside window is an invitation. Layer clean sheets, loose blankets, and fresh laundry over the bed. Bury us within it—bury us within a sable sky.

> NOTE: Spines are a body-map, and fingers are footsteps.

Walk all over me. Dig your iron-clad boots into my neck. Don't ask me any questions. Tell me I'm a good woman. Grind your sandpaper cheek against my chin till it's raw and splintering. I don't mind. Grip my inner thigh with your teeth, and tell me how it feels to taste a blue-blood moon. Tell your friends you're tired and bored.

> NOTE: "Intimidating" is a marriage between a ghost and
> fantasy within your body.

III.

After she draped a layer of spring over her shoulders, she pestled petals with her teeth, and spit insight into their mouths. They abandoned their towers, took moss as a second skin. Pleasure was an absence of the lord's blue-black handprint around their necks. They ran to her.

> NOTE: A mind-disease is a narrative, and she was a healer.

In the end the lord will offer her a seat at his right hand.
In the end she will ask for everything.
In the end they will burn her.

IV.
It is not enough to simply leave her alone.

> NOTE: "Leaving" is a deep breath of Redwood air.

V.
Eggshell walls foreground the shadows of braided bodies. The television runs without eyes to lie across the pane. Whatever bruises the body remembers melt away under his tongue. Flesh, to flesh, to fabric, to the looming fear of wanting something she can't give. A film left by heavy breath crawls up the window in slow centimeters—
then dissolves.

VI.
Tell me you imagine me naked in a field of snow.

VII.
Sand mingles with her fingertips. Her hand presses deeper into the earth until the echo of the tide becomes tangible. He fractures silence with a monologue of unmet desires.
When will the tide open its mouth and beg?

> NOTE: "She" is wood-pulp, bleached and flattened into a white sheet, his hand hovering above the surface, a drop of red hanging from the paintbrush.

Figure, Oil on Canvas, a Mirror

Splayed out on a palette,
      the meadowed neck facing
heaven,   or some other
      kind place.
Sparingly,   I see the canyons
of Moab ripple through her
legs,   which rest,   bent,
the way fire tricks you into
      thinking it is   stagnant, or fluid,
or something other than energy.
      The river—the disturbed desert
          —runs down her calf,
suggesting it once ran between her thighs.
      Her clavicle   rises inches above
      her chest: hooked,   unbroken,
      her ribs: reinforced,   rebar,
      her sternum: an amphitheater
          for the belly.
Observers pour over her organs—
sing praises   of the body's
      second chorus.
      She is silver and glass.
      I want to reach for her—to press
my bloody nose   into her
      indigo fingertips, to be violet
on a violent canvas,
      to be one step closer than Adam,
    the way some creator intended.
But, I've been tricked again.
      I cannot drape the colors
         over our bare body.

To the Ants in my Kitchen

I want to be held down. I don't know what to do with the horrifying freedom that will destroy me.
      —   *Clarice Lispector, The Passion According to G.H.*

When some god grows hungry for wetness, for water and more water, or a darkness that soaks through my skin, my countertop is heaven for an hour. The door will be cracked open. Thick air will pour through it. I will hold a glass in my right hand and not itch when I look at you. Even as you litter my countertops as commas and periods in my thoughts, I will lather my throat with hot water. Even while you examine the gatherings of dead daisies on my shelves, or hung against my walls, I will look out the window and hope you find some comfort. I will say *Thank you for coming.* I will make the foods my mother didn't teach me to make. The wind will press a young pine into itself and I will sit upright. I will put the dish rag in the washing machine, and not imagine crushing you within the terry-woven cloth. I will turn off the house lights, and try not to catch you, or the small bread crumbs I have left on the pan the cutting board the floor, or the lemon juice mingled with curacao or my mother's notes on how to wash a silk shirt or fragments of tobacco leaves or the ticket stub from the last time I let a man say *thank you for having me* or the mango rinds next to a bowl of uneaten fruit or the whiskey I drank after the curaçao or the peanut butter spoon or the medications next to the vitamins next to the kitchen knife next to my sink which has been dripping for so long—so incessantly.

Three Rivers: Fawn Head Mantle

Rivers, diverging at the precipice of Sequoias and Redwoods.
Trees are witnesses; stretching their bodies wide, speaking
in long low tones, taking years to say a single word. You and I
have outpaced all that is necessary to say, and so we speak like trees.

Bits of metal dig into the cavities in our molars, beneath a day-old
cherry pie. You don't mind. On a Heineken-soaked wooden chair, I
collect my adult body into itself. A fawn's head hangs on the wall
of the cafe. I want to spit out my food. I don't want to disappoint you.

Outside the window, a river streams beneath a small bridge.
Mallard ducks land where the water pools and slows. They dip
their bills into the winter runoff. You look down, smiling.
The pie between us is breaking down along the edge of a fork.

I rest, and you peruse my forearm with your fingertips, running
them along flesh that resembles bark more than skin. You mention
how, when we're apart, you think of how your lips feel when you
kiss my forehead after I shower. I stay quiet and soak in the water.

For a moment, I forget the fawn's head looming over me. The phrase,
"when I was young" becomes a fired bullet, resting in a bed of pine
needles. I forget the wound. It is only a line you trace with kindness.

We are here, and I am soft. You hold me like my bones don't live
                                                    in the riverbed.

Bone Hunting

Stepping into the dry mouth of the
    riverbed. Filled with calcitic trees,
        undertones of pheasant pie,
           rotting velvet pears
              from the garden.

He's picking his teeth with a bird rib,
    kicking up dust clouds with his canvas shoes,
while I try to dig my arrowhead into a young pine.

    For two weeks in July I'm playing farm boy,
        hunter,   explorer.

His 10-year-old fingers flex and fold around the antlers
    that grow out of the summer sand;
        he exhumes the splintered horns,
            root and stem.

Piles of fractured femurs,
    severed spines,
        ulnas, clavicles
lie beside shallow pits left in the earth.

I turn away from him,
    draw,
        aim
He says it's hunting season.
    We're too young to hold a gun.
        As if our fathers weren't children.
    Again, I shoot,
        missing,
           running,
              picking up my single arrow.

A lone stag strides
    out of the surrounding woods
    —broad shouldered, towering
        over the gravesite.

```
         Speckled fur hugs its calves, stomach, neck,
                lays still against its infrastructure.
         There is a breath—the belly extending,
                the silent exhale,
                a return to home.
It surveys the punctures in the ground,
                and the two farm boys
         who thought they'd discovered it.

I pull the drawstring back.
                My arrowhead lingers on the stag's oak-neck.
                     I know his antlers have scarred tissue,
                          have broken apart the landscape.

The string's tension rings in my ears,
         and I stare into his eyes—
         within them, I see:
                flickers of amber, corn-husk suns,
                     and South Dakota plains.

I lower my gangling arms, and step down;
         the stag departs into the shadowed woods,

         and the farm boy tells me
                how I could've killed him,
                     if I wanted to.
```

Here and There

"There" is a reckoning:

    an unwritten elegy,
        oak-roots swelling against
        the ruptured sidewalk,
a bile-stained rag coupled with
        vindication,
an infection,
        a hospital,
Redwood bodies on the truck bed,
        laid to rest on the hillside,
the recurrent absence of sound—
        self-inflicted,
self-centered,
        self-indulgent,
a meal untouched,
        my thoughts meandering
            around your body,
a detour from your voice,
        soil brushed over the casket,
soil rendered infertile,
        my hermetic rendition of
        life,
        my apartment empty,
blood on the doorway,
        an unrecognizable face in
        a pool of
saliva and bourbon,
a deer gnawing at every sapling
        till starvation,
and a thick bottom line
        if I choose to follow you.

            ……

"Here" is a guilt:

    a howling,
        a thought unspoken,
    a garden tucked in the city's
        hillside pocket,
    a birthday where
        I turn older than you,
    a birthday where
        I turn 21,
    a beer belly
        looming above
            the boxer brief,
    a pill bug crawling up
        the doghouse,
    a cotton-voice calling me
        back to bed,
    an end to a 5-year drought,
    a kiss shared
        by a stranger,
    a kiss from the woman I love,
        a promise kept,
    a guitar restrung
        and re-tuned,
    a wider set of hips,
        a reminder of absence,
    a ball of snow encased in
            pink-red fingers,
    a fire in the neighborhood
        that smells like your coat,
    a morning where I dip peanut-butter
        cookies into my coffee,
    a tear-stained pillow,
        a set of boat sails,
    a flush from being called beautiful,
        a homegrown meal,
    a man at the cafe who smiled
        with his top lip,
    a man I could have sworn was you.

Mount Washington: Rain for the Departing

Between a father's hands
    (before he casts down a fruit fly
    onto the granite countertop)
        sits a capillary meadow.

The moment begins,
    you hear the car before it turns around
        the dampened bend and into sight.

The fresh grass,
    undulating hairs that embrace the forearm,
        breathe once more.
    Chattering. Swinging for
        a higher branch. Falling.

The worm, revived as if it was a newborn,
    moves without the need for legs
        across the silken pavement.

The wounds left by the flatbed truck renew
    as a collection of watering holes
        for the starlings.

(Time sustains. The root chord on
    a Yamaha. The words on
    the page as they take your
    shape.)

The rocks, once homogenous,
    have presented themselves
        as nutmeg, hazelnuts, charcoal.

The black walnut tree has appeared again,
    mutilated in our own image,
        encroaching as a Bauhaus ceiling.

*(Orange light appears from a window. The
                view of an orchard from a moving car.
                Iodine glazing the flesh of a house.)*

The atmosphere drags down
            from what is left of your
                        forehead and your lips.

The path downhill is a coin and a lattice river,
            meant to be traversed by a body
                        that does not know itself.

The sky is not crying.
            *Your shadow might be
                        crying over my shoulder*
                        It is likely the clouds
                                    simply stood still.

Kiss by the Window

Edvard Munch, 1892

The lyrics of the dogwood
        litter themselves across
        blurred shoulders.
Seedlings,
          embedded in the sidewalk,
          reach their tender hands,
              open wide,
                  beg for another mouthful of sun.
Night remains unyielding.
              The window shields nothing.
A man slides his tongue
        around the rim of a glass
        and straight into her heart.
Drinking down honeycomb
          slathered in rice wine,
          descending like silver coins.
Who knows what else he has hidden in his mouth,
    between his teeth,   in the words
                you're beautiful.
She remembers:
        making love to an odor,
        the collarbone shelf where her chin rested
                        and fell,
        the piano keys she pressed
            when she was young and impressive
                in that quiet way;
    someone
        who tore her linen
           with his eyes,
           then his hands,
    the morning glory that
        died after its first bloom.

A moment of oblivion
        seeps into his lips.
Even the metaphor of death
    cannot be reasoned with.

Delivering the End

I.

What comes to mind is mornings, you say. Liquid sun staining the bed. Legs more liquid than light. My eyes: more green than brown. Your eyes: more brown than green. Our mouths only make the same shape when they kiss.

II.

Birds cooing like a shoulder tap, like an alarm. Arguments sticking between teeth—5 things I love about you. Spinach on rye bread, chlorophyll languages grumbling down the throat, the belly, the creaking house. A pictureless puzzle—a knife, a back, a dripping answer.

III.

I tell you about the boneyard to tell you about violence. You hear a trial woven into the landscape. I hear a truth that can't surpass the page.

IV.

Do you see what I mean? I say. Here are 5 ways he is like my father. Here are 5 ways he is like his father. The will to change spliced with a chest-ache, with the act of hanging up the phone. Good woman, come home. Here are 5 ways I am like my mother. Embodying a witness, a lover, a teacher, and a loser so he can sleep well tonight.

V.

The day-bed in Bellingham. Hanging off the edge of the mattress. Solar-flare in the living room. Wisps of hair—flames scorching your pink cheeks. Scanning your freckles for stars, or seeds. Thumbing my cheek while we hide underneath the covers. The aftermath of hard rain fogging up the window. Returning here—like an act of forgiveness.

Thank you Mom and Dad for letting me be a poet instead of a businessman.

Thank you Sarah Maclay, Julia Lee, and Gail Wronsky for all of your support throughout this writing process. It is such an honor to learn from such prolific writers.

Thank you Audrey for your artistry, and even more for your friendship.

Trinity Catlin (they/she) is a queer Filipino poet who is currently completing their MA in English at Loyola Marymount university.

They have served as the co-head editor of the student-led publication LA Miscellany, and have been published in LA Miscellany, Attic Salt, Sunstroke magazine, and Beyond Queer Words.

They are also the recipient of the Leonard Simon Blenkiron Award, and the Knott Fellowship.

Also Available from Cathexis Northwest Press:

Something To Cry About
by Robert Krantz

Suburban Hermeneutics
by Ian Cappelli

God's Love Is Very Busy
by David Seung

that one time we were almost people
by Christian Czaniecki

Fever Dream/Take Heart
by Valyntina Grenier

The Book of Night & Waking
by Clif Mason

Dead Birds of New Zealand
by Christian Czaniecki

The Weathering of Igneous Rockforms in High-Altitude Riparian Environments
by John Belk

If A Fish
by George Burns

How to Draw a Blank
by Collin Van Son

En Route
by Jesse Wolfe

sky bright psalms
by Temple Cone

Moonbird
by Henry G. Stanton

southern athiest. oh, honey
by d. e. fulford

Bruises, Birthmarks & Other Calamities
by Nadine Klassen

Wanted: Comedy, Addicts
by AR Dugan

They Curve Like Snakes
by David Alexander McFarland

the catalog of daily fears
by Beth Dufford

Shops Close Too Early
by Josh Feit

Vanity Unfair and Other Poems
by Robert Eugene Rubino

Destructive Heresies
by Milo E. Gorgevska

Bodies of Separation
by Chim Sher Ting

The Night with James Dean and Other Prose Poems
by Allison A. deFreese

About Time
by Julie Benesh

Suspended
by Ellen White Rook

The Unempty Spaces Between
by Louis Efron

Quomodo probatur in conflatorio
by Nick Roberts

Suspended
by Ellen White Rook

Call Me Not Ishmael but the Sea
by J. Martin Daughtry

Wild Evolution
by Naomi Leimsider

Coming To Terms
by Peter Sagnella

Acta
by Patrick Wilcox

Honeymoon Shoes
by Valyntina Grenier

Practising Ascending
by Nadine Hitchiner

Home Visit
by Michal Rubin

LA CIUDAD EN TI: THE CITY WITHIN YOU
by Karla Marrufo
Translated from the Spanish by Allison A. deFreese

Resin in the Milky Way
by Amanda Rabaduex

Rabbit Hole
by Crystal Ignatowski

Muskets for the Bear Problem
by Andrew Whitmer

Cathexis Northwest Press

www.ingramcontent.com/pod-product-compliance
Lightning Source LLC
Chambersburg PA
CBHW011407070526
44586CB00022B/2596